I0886605

12 THINGS TO KNOW ABOUT THE BRONZE AGE

by Meg Marquardt

12 STORY LIBRARY
MORE TO EXPLORE

www.12StoryLibrary.com

Copyright © 2020 by 12-Story Library, Mankato, MN 56002. All rights reserved. No part of this book may be reproduced or utilized in any form or by any means without written permission from the publisher.

12-Story Library is an imprint of Bookstaves.

Photographs ©: Michael Ebardt/Shutterstock.com, cover, 1; James William Smith/Shutterstock.com, 4; Southern Vadim/Shutterstock.com, 5; Morphart Creation/Shutterstock.com, 6; johzio/Shutterstock.com, 7; fotopanorama360/Shutterstock.com, 8; BabelStone/CC3.0, 9; peacefoo/Shutterstock.com, 10; 3DF mediaStudio/Shutterstock.com, 11; Bjørn Christian Tørrissen/CC3.0, 11; Osama Shukir Muhammed Amin FRCP/CC4.0, 12; Mbzt/CC3.0, 13; jsp/Shutterstock.com, 13; Bernard Gagnon/CC3.0, 14; Skreidzeleu/Shutterstock.com, 15; R.F. Morgan/CC3.0, 15; Anagoria/CC3.0, 16; PD, 17; Matjaž Kacicnik/University of Basel, 18; Stzeman/CC3.0, 19; Dmitry V. Petrenko/Shutterstock.com, 20; C messier/CC4.0, 21; Jada Images/Alamy, 22; B.O'Kane/Alamy, 23; PD, 24; Ivy Close Images/Alamy, 25; Carole Raddato/CC2.0, 26; Alexikoua/CC3.0, 27; Roland Unger/CC3.0, 29

ISBN
9781632357663 (hardcover)
9781632358752 (paperback)
9781645820482 (ebook)

Library of Congress Control Number: 2019938634

Printed in the United States of America
July 2019

About the Cover
Tools from the Bronze Age.

Access free, up-to-date content on this topic plus a full digital version of this book. Scan the QR code on page 31 or use your school's login at 12StoryLibrary.com.

Table of Contents

1 Change Happened at Different Times in Different Places

A fortress and settlement in Tel Arad, Israel, that dates back to the Bronze Age.

A few centuries before the Bronze Age, people lived in small communities. They only used stone tools. They had just learned how to grow crops. All that was about to change.

Just like the name suggests, the Bronze Age started when people began using bronze to make tools. The Bronze Age was a time of growth. It stretched from around 3300 to 1200 BCE (Before the Common Era). Years BCE are counted backwards. The Common Era (CE) starts with the birth of Jesus of Nazareth. After that, years are counted forward. We live around 2000 CE. This means the Bronze Age began around 5,300 years ago and ended about 3,200 years ago.

That seems like a really long time. But the Bronze Age was similar to the Common Era in many ways. People were starting to live in big cities ruled by a central government. They were better farmers. Bronze tools are stronger than stone tools and last longer. Farmers could be more efficient. They could grow food for more people. That left time for other people to pursue other jobs and interests. Religion, medicine, and science all grew.

Not all areas entered the Bronze Age at the same time. The Middle East and Egypt started right around 3300 BCE. But places like China didn't enter the Bronze Age until 1700 BCE. In some places, the Bronze Age began even later. Eventually, people all over the Old World—Africa, Asia and Europe—were using the metal.

87 percent

Amount of copper in a bronze weapon

- The rest was mostly tin.
- There were also traces of other elements like iron and nickel.
- The earliest bronze weapons came out of Egypt in 4000 BCE. The Middle East was also discovering bronze at this time.

An assortment of tools from the Bronze Age unearthed in Siberia.

2 People Crafted Metal Tools and Weapons

Learning to make bronze tools and weapons was quite a feat. Bronze is a mix of copper and tin. Copper is soft. Adding tin makes it stronger. When two metals are combined, it is called an alloy. Bronze was one of the first and most important alloys of the ancient world.

Copper and tin were mined and traded. Metalsmiths would heat them and mix them together. They would pour the liquid metal into molds made of sand or clay. After the metal cooled, they would break the molds and remove the tools or weapons.

Smiths used bronze to make new kinds of weapons. Swords began to dominate warfare. A sword made of stone wouldn't be practical. But a bronze sword is lighter and sturdier. Smiths made swords in different shapes and sizes. A sword might be shaped like a sickle. A sickle is a curved blade. Or it might start out thick by the handle and get thinner and sharper at the end.

Weapons from the period have been discovered in tombs of warriors.

As weapons got better, warriors needed more protection. Metalsmiths also made armor from bronze. Warriors went into battle wearing bronze breastplates and helmets. They carried bronze shields. They fought with bronze swords and threw bronze spears.

METEOR METAL

Some tools from the Bronze Age were made of iron. This puzzled scientists. Humans didn't know how to make iron in the Bronze Age. When scientists analyzed the weapons, they learned something surprising. The tools were made of metal from meteorites. Bronze Age people weren't making iron. They had just found a secret stash from space.

4,000

Estimated number of warriors who fought in a fierce Bronze Age battle

- The battle took place in Germany around 1250 BCE.
- Bones of men and horses have been found, along with weapons and armor.
- Researchers are surprised by the size of the battle and how organized it was.

3

Empires Grew in Size and Power

The Bronze Age was the time of the first great empires. Empires are a type of government system. They contain large cities or city-states. A city-state is an early version of a country. Armies from the city or city-state would go out and invade new lands. The more land an empire conquered, the larger and more powerful it grew.

One area was full of Bronze Age empires. Its name was Mesopotamia. It was located in the Middle East. Two rivers flowed through it, the Tigris and the Euphrates. Both were important trade routes. All along their banks, cities cropped up. Some of those cities grew into empires. Some of the most famous were the Assyrian

Ancient ruins of Dara, a city in Mesopotamia.

This pottery version of the game 58 Holes dates from 1290 BCE.

PLAYING GAMES

Bronze Age people created new types of entertainment. One example is a 4,000-year-old board game. The game was called 58 Holes. It was sort of like Chutes and Ladders. The goal was to get a peg to the end space. Some of the pegs were carved to look like jackals or monkeys.

Empire, the Babylonian Empire, the Sumerian Empire, and Mari.

China also had empires. These empires were dynasties. A dynasty means that rulers come from the same family. A son will rule after his father, and on and on. In China, the major dynasties were the Shang and Zhou dynasties. The Shang made intricate pieces of bronze art. Large vessels were decorated with raised, stylized animal faces known as *taotie*.

12

Number of city-states in the Sumerian Empire in 3000 BCE

- One important city-state was Uruk. It would later become part of Iraq.
- The *Epic of Gilgamesh* dates from around 2000 BCE. It may be the world's oldest surviving work of great literature. It was written about a king of Uruk.
- The people of Uruk built temples called ziggurats. They look like pyramids made of steps.

4 Bronze Age People Wrote Using Pictures and Symbols

Hieroglyphs cover most of the inside walls of the tomb of Ramesses VI in Egypt.

Archaeologists know a lot more about Bronze Age culture than any culture that came before. That's because many Bronze Age cultures had some kind of writing. The writing doesn't look like writing today. Instead of letters, it might have symbols or pictures.

Ancient Egyptian hieroglyphs are a famous type of early writing. Hieroglyphs are images that stand for words or sounds. For example, the image of a reed might represent the sound "I." But the reed could also be used to represent an object, such as a plant. Hieroglyphs were often written top to bottom rather than side to side.

Ancient writing also appeared in India. The Indus script is an example of a form of writing that hasn't yet been translated. Archaeologists know how to read Egyptian hieroglyphs. They had help from something called the Rosetta Stone. But they don't know how to read Indus script. That's because no translation tool has ever been found. Another problem is very few examples of Indus script have

3
Languages on the Rosetta Stone

- The Rosetta Stone was discovered in 1799 near Alexandria, Greece.
- It has the same words written in three languages: Egyptian hieroglyphics, Egyptian demotic, and Greek.
- People already knew how to read Greek. With the discovery of the Rosetta Stone, they had a key to translate hieroglyphs, too.

The Rosetta Stone.

been discovered. Researchers think that most examples were written on leaves or bark. They haven't survived.

Another example of early writing is Sumerian cuneiform. Cuneiform looks like a bunch of triangles and squares arranged in different ways. Sumerian writers would use a pointed tool called a stylus to draw lines on soft clay. Many clay tablets survive today.

THINK ABOUT IT

Imagine that something you write will last for thousands of years. It all has to fit on a clay tablet. What will you write?

This cuneiform inscription dates back 25 centuries.

5

Bronze Age Societies Needed Rules and Laws

Bronze Age cities had complex social structures. A social structure is the way a society is organized. It determines the rules people live by and how they behave. It defines who has what kind of status and why. Everyone has a role to play.

The Bronze Age chiefdoms of Scandinavia are one example of a social structure. Chiefdoms were smaller than empires. But they still had a complex society. Each chief was in charge of about 300 people, from farmers to warriors. The chief would make sure that supplies were shared equally. Archaeologists think chiefdoms often broke apart when their leader died. They reformed when a new leader took over.

In big cities, different social structures were appearing. People were starting to make complex laws. One example is the Code of Hammurabi. This set of laws was written under King Hammurabi of Babylonia. He ruled from 1792 BCE to 1750 BCE. The laws were written on a stone pillar 7½ feet (2.25 m) high. The pillar was discovered in 1901.

The code has 282 laws. Some of the laws have to do with trade. Others have to do with crimes, such as attacking

King Hammurabi raises his right arm in worship on this limestone carving.

10

Silver shekels a doctor in Babylonia could charge to heal a rich person's wound

- This was according to the Code of Hammurabi. The Code laid out how much certain things cost.
- Silver shekels were a form of money in Babylonia.
- The doctor could only charge two shekels to heal a slave's wound.

another person. The laws are a snapshot of Babylonian life. For example, if someone attacked a slave, the person might just have to pay a fine. But if someone attacked a rich person, the punishment could be much harsher. The attacker's hands might be cut off. This tells us something about the social structure of Babylonia.

The Code of Hammurabi pillar was found by archeologists in 1901 while excavating the ancient city of Susa, which is in modern-day Iran.

THINK ABOUT IT

Why do societies need rules and laws? What would life be like without rules and laws?

6 Architecture Was about Art and Practicality

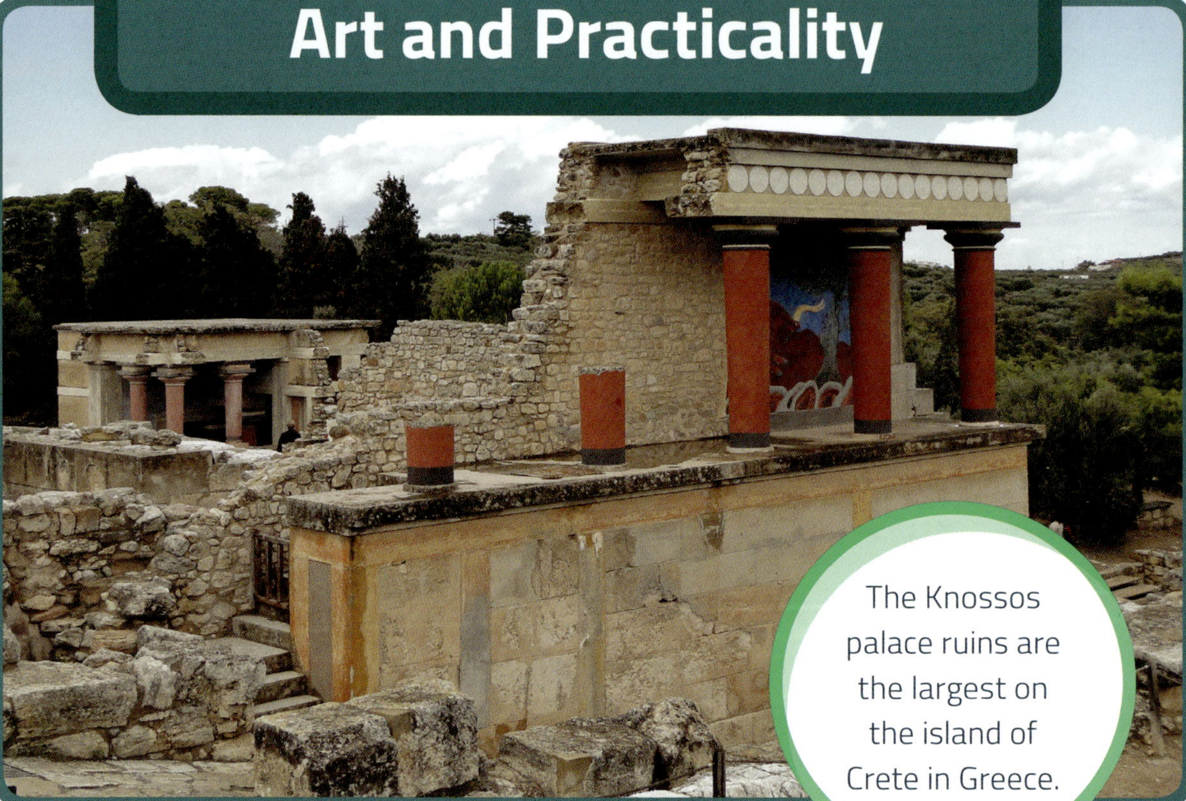

The Knossos palace ruins are the largest on the island of Crete in Greece.

The Bronze Age saw a new wave of architecture. Architecture is part science and part art. A building needs to be sturdy. It needs to stand safely for a long time in all kinds of weather. But a building can also be beautiful.

Greek architects built stunning palaces. Over a third of the space was used for storage. Researchers have found hoards of stone tablets. They have found containers for food and drink. Some of the palaces were four stories high. They would have been a lot taller than surrounding buildings.

The palaces were built mostly from large sandstone bricks. They were built in phases over a period of years. Different builders might have taken over at different times. As a

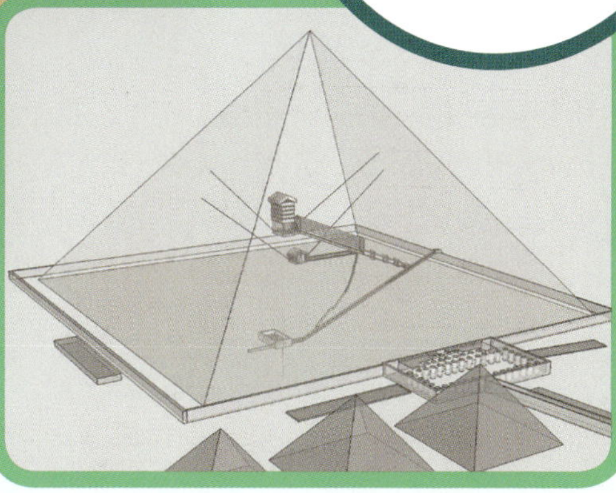

The Great Pyramid of Giza, also known as Khufu's pyramid.

result, some palaces had confusing structures. Some had so many rooms they were like giant mazes. Architects in ancient Egypt were thinking even bigger. The rulers of Egypt were called pharaohs. They built huge tombs for themselves. Tombs are vaults used to bury the dead. Egyptian rulers built giant pyramids. One of the largest is the Great Pyramid of Giza. It was built for a pharaoh named Khufu. He died in 2567 BCE. His pyramid is 481 feet (148 m) tall. That's almost 50 stories.

7 Wonders of the Ancient World

- The Seven Wonders are great architectural feats.
- Khufu's pyramid is one of the wonders. It is the only Bronze Age wonder.
- Other wonders are the Hanging Gardens of Babylon and the statue of Zeus at Olympia in Greece.

WHO BUILT THE PYRAMIDS?

There were slaves in Egypt. Some were criminals forced to work without pay. Others were people captured in a battle. But slaves probably didn't build the pyramids. That is a myth. Researchers think that lower-class workers built them.

7 The Bronze Age Was the Beginning of Science

Bronze Age science didn't look like modern science. There were no laboratories or people in white lab coats. In the Bronze Age, science was just starting out. Almost all the great scientific discoveries hadn't been made yet. The word "scientist" didn't even exist and wouldn't for thousands of years.

One area early scientists worked on a lot is astronomy. Astronomy is the study of the stars and other heavenly bodies. These scientists didn't know that stars were big balls of gas. But they did know that the bright dots in the night sky seemed to move.

Early scientists created objects like the Nebra sky disk. The disk was found in 1999 by treasure hunters using a metal detector. It was discovered about 160 miles (256 km) southwest of Berlin, Germany.

The Nebra sky disc is about 12 inches in diamter (32 cm) and weighs 4.4 pounds (2 kg).

The Pleiades cluster is 400 light-years (122 parsecs) from Earth.

7
Stars in the Pleiades cluster on the Nebra sky disk

- The Pleiades rise and set in the night sky. They are visible from almost everywhere on earth. Many ancient civilizations used them as a calendar.
- On the Nebra sky disk, the Pleiades are shown as a group of seven stars. That's how most people see them with the naked eye.
- In reality, the Pleiades contain hundreds of stars.

It dates from around 1600 BCE. The disk is green and blue. It is covered with gold stars and different phases of the moon. Researchers aren't certain what it was used for. But one guess is it helped farmers know when to plant their crops. It is like an astronomical calendar.

Bronze Age people looked at the stars for another reason. Today, astrology is considered a pseudoscience. Modern experts don't think it's very scientific. But in the Bronze Age, astrology was taken very seriously. Astrology uses the stars to predict the future. Believers think the way stars move paints a picture of things to come.

8

Different Areas Practiced Different Types of Medicine

New types of medical treatment emerged in the Bronze Age. One was the use of prosthetics. Prosthetics are used to replace a limb or other body part. For example, if a person loses a toe to an injury, they can get a prosthetic toe to replace it. One of the first prosthetics was actually a toe. A 3,000-year-old toe was found in Egypt. Some researchers think a metal hand found in Switzerland is an example of Bronze Age prosthetics.

Different parts of the world came up with different medical practices. People living in today's India developed Ayurveda. This used a vast system of plants and minerals for healing. Poems called *shlokas* described how to use the plants. Ayurveda is still practiced today as a traditional form of medicine.

Ancient Egypt had advanced medical practices. Egyptians believed in cleanliness. They washed tools that

The 3,000-year-old prosthethic toe was found on a female mummy in an ancient Egyptian grave site.

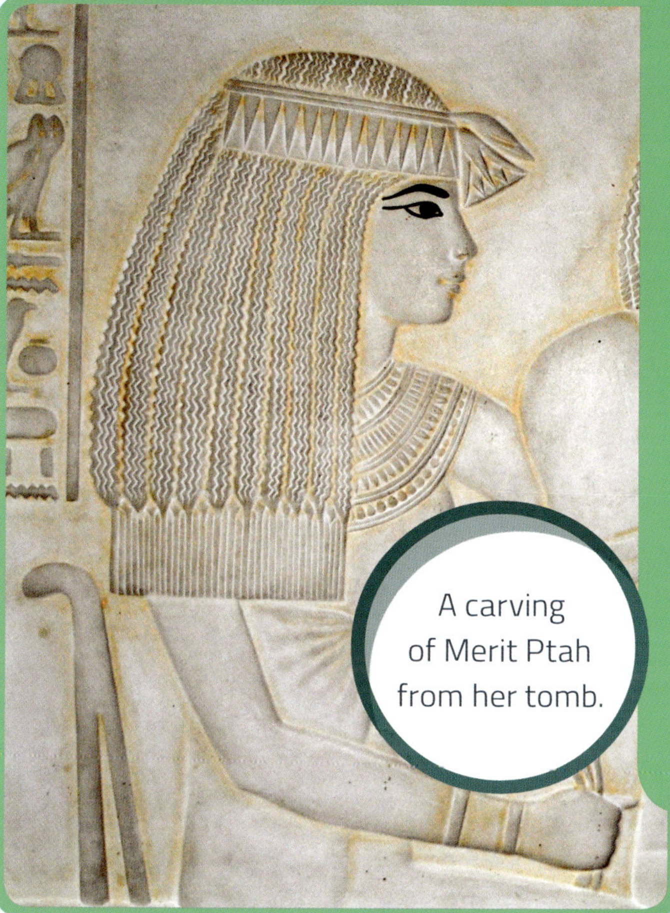

A carving of Merit Ptah from her tomb.

Around 2700 BCE

Time when Merit Ptah practiced medicine in Egypt

- She was one of the world's first female doctors.
- A description on her tomb calls her the "chief physician."
- She likely taught other doctors working in the royal court.

were used to treat wounds. Other cultures didn't take that step, so infection was a problem for them. Ancient Egyptians also thought diseases were punishments from the gods, or demon possession. They used spells and magic to try to drive disease away.

BRONZE AGE DISEASES

Even though the Bronze Age was 5,000 years ago, diseases then were a lot like diseases today. People died of cancer and heart disease. They also suffered from diseases that don't exist anymore. People in ancient Egypt died of smallpox. Smallpox was eradicated in 1979.

9

New Religions Were Created

With so many civilizations arising in the Bronze Age, it's not surprising that many religions popped up, too. Researchers have learned a lot about some ancient religions.

For the ancient Egyptians, religion was a huge part of everyday life. Egyptians had many religious rituals, festivals, and temples. They followed a big group of gods and

2,000
Gods in the ancient Egyptian pantheon

- Bastet was the goddess of home and of cats.
- Amenet would greet people who had just entered the afterlife.
- Amun-Ra was the god of the sun.

Sculpture of Osiris at entrance to a temple in Egypt.

goddesses called a pantheon. They believed in the afterlife and made elaborate preparations for it. When a person died, everything but the heart was removed from the body. Then the body was embalmed and mummified. The Egyptians believed the god Osiris would weigh their heart in the underworld. If their heart passed the test, they would be allowed to enter paradise.

In Greece, the Minoans had their own pantheon. Theirs was much smaller. There was a central female goddess. In statues and pictures, she is often surrounded by snakes or holding snakes. Researchers sometimes call her the Mother Goddess or the Snake Goddess. Bulls were also important to Minoan religion. They were often offered up as sacrifices to the gods.

In ancient China, people believed in ghosts as well as gods. Ghosts were the spirits of people who had died. People became ghosts if they didn't live a good life. They also became ghosts if their surviving relatives didn't take care of their tombs. Chinese people today still practice care for ancient ancestors. It's thought that deceased family members can intervene with the gods on behalf of the living.

The snakes are meant to convey power and strength.

10

The Wheel Hit the Scene

Archaeologists uncovered this 3,000 year-old Bronze Age wheel in England in 2016.

The wheel was first used for pottery. A potter's wheel is a wheel laid on its side. It is spun very quickly and pottery is made on top of it. A skilled potter can make something that has smooth, even sides. The potter's wheel was invented in Mesopotamia around 3500 BCE.

Hundreds of years would go by before someone put a wheel on a vehicle. The first wheeled object

3

Size in feet (1 m) of the largest Bronze Age wheel discovered to date

- The wheel was found in Britain.
- It dates from around 1000 BCE.
- It was probably part of a two-wheeled cart that was pulled by oxen.

ROLLING ALONG

Humans were building large structures before the wheel was invented. So how did they get all their materials in one place? They still used things that rolled. They might put a large stone block on long tree trunks laid side-by-side. Then they would use ropes to pull the block along over the trunks.

might have been a wheelbarrow. A wheelbarrow is a cart a person pushes. Imagine being a Bronze Age construction worker. You would have to move supplies like mud from one area to another. Without a cart, you would have to lug around a bucket.

Wheels changed the way people worked.

Eventually, wheels ended up on vehicles. Egyptians rode in chariots. Chariots are platforms with wheels. A person could stand on the platform. A horse or pair of horses would pull the platform along.

The world's oldest known wooden wheel was found in Slovenia in 2002. Researchers believe it dates back to about 3200 BCE. It is 27½ inches (70 cm) wide and 2 inches (5 cm) thick. Archaeologists found it in marshes about 12 miles (20 km) south of the city of Ljubljana. It is known as the Ljubljana Marshes Wheel.

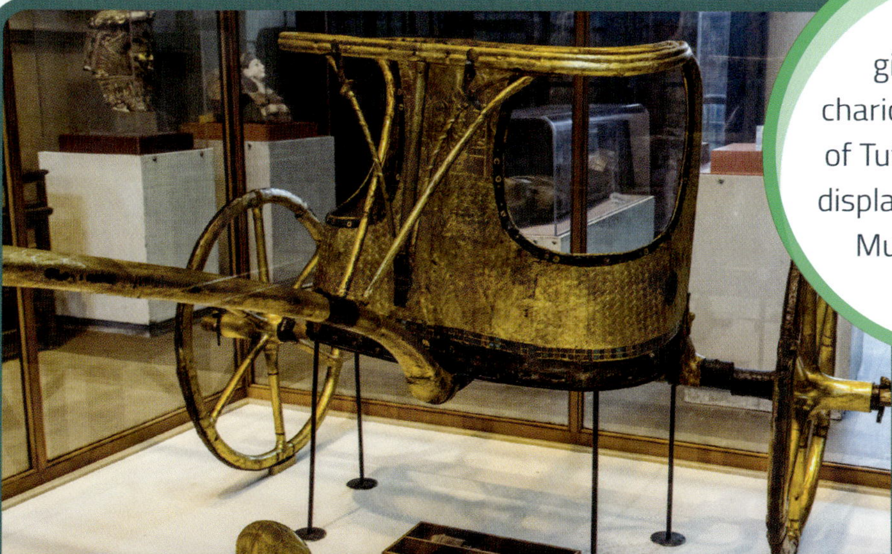

The gilded wooden chariot from the tomb of Tutankhamun is on display at the Egyphan Museum in Cairo, Egypt.

11 Trade Began Close to Home and Far Away

With the invention of the wheel, Bronze Age people had places to go. Roads were also getting better. Some trading took place on the local level. This probably happened well before the start of the Bronze Age. People were growing crops, raising animals, and making pottery. They could have traded these for other goods.

Trade routes popped up in the Middle East. Along these routes, towns started to form. These were like the world's first rest stops. Merchants would travel along the roads. They would stop at towns that had inns where they could sleep. They would move from town to town. These merchants could carry their goods a long way. There were trade routes that connected the Middle East to Greece, Egypt, and China.

Merchants worked from early morning to sunset buying and selling goods.

People weren't only traveling on land. They were also using water to trade goods. Some

50,000

Number of tools found near a tin mine in the Middle East

- Researchers once thought most of the tin in the Middle East was imported.
- The mine is located in today's Turkey.
- It suggests that tin mining was well under way by the start of the Bronze Age.

LITTLE MINERS

Bronze was made of tin and copper. Both had to be mined. Tunnels and shafts had to be dug out of stone using stone hammers. It was hard work, and it took a lot of time. So tunnels ended up being small. Some are so small that researchers think children did much of the work underground. There weren't any schools to go to, so they worked, just like adults.

went down rivers like the Nile. Other Bronze Age travelers took to the sea. For example, people from Ireland were trading gold with people in Britain.

This limestone relief from 1570-1292 BCE shows cargo ships unloading their goods at port.

12 The Bronze Age Collapsed Unexpectedly

The Bronze Age was a time of great growth. Cities got bigger. New rulers created sprawling empires. There were advances in science, medicine, and religion. But suddenly, it all came to a stop.

Around 1200 BCE, the Bronze Age mysteriously collapsed. This happened around the Mediterranean Sea. Early Greek, Egyptian, and Middle Eastern societies just stopped thriving. To this day, researchers aren't quite sure what happened.

One theory suggests there was a major drought. Drought happens where there isn't any rain. The land gets really dry. It's hard to grow crops. Without crops, large cities can't feed their citizens. Without food, all those great advances in civilization don't mean a lot. People would have left their homes. Whole cities would have disappeared.

Another theory says that a mysterious group of people invaded. Researchers today call them the Sea Peoples. They sailed in and attacked. They might have come from Europe or other parts of Asia. They might have destroyed whole cities.

The Bronze Age collapse probably happened because of a combination of things.

Archaeologists believe this temple in Amman Jordan was never finished at the end of the Bronze Age.

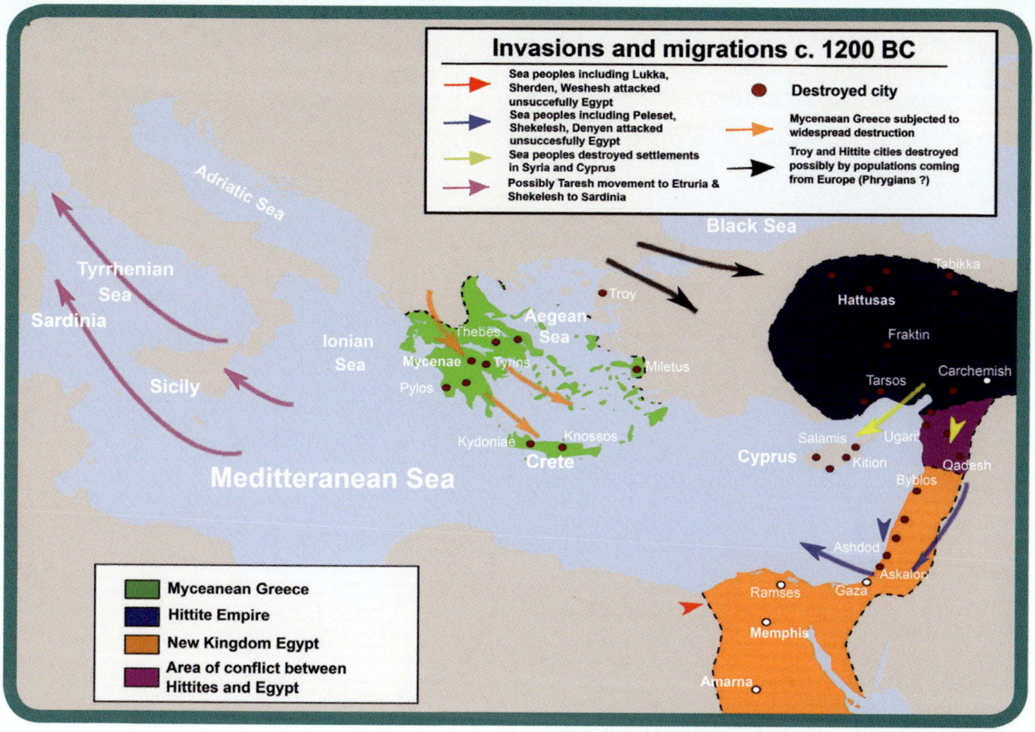

Researchers have evidence that drought was a problem. They also have ancient documents that detail the invasion of the Sea Peoples. These problems were happening at the same time. It was too much for some cities to survive. The Bronze Age ended quickly. A dark age began. But humanity would live on.

THINK ABOUT IT

Researchers keep trying to find out why the Bronze Age collapsed. The collapse happened a very long time ago. Why is it important to know more about it?

150

Years the drought lasted during the Bronze Age collapse

- Researchers looked at pollen samples from various points in time in Israel.
- The samples showed there was a sharp decline in the number of trees in the region.
- The lack of trees is a sign of a major drought.

Timeline of the Bronze Age

The Bronze Age lasted from around 5,300 years ago to 3,200 years ago.

5,300 years ago:
People start to use bronze tools and weapons.

4,600 years ago:
The Old Kingdom of Egypt begins.

4,500 years ago:
Workers are carving the Great Sphinx in Egypt.

4,000 years ago:
People are playing the game 58 Holes.

3,700 years ago:
The Code of Hammurabi is written.

3,600 years ago:
The eruption of Thera, a volcano on the island of Santorini, changes the ancient world.

3,330 years ago:
King Tutankhamen rules Egypt.

3,200 years ago:
The Bronze Age suddenly collapses. No one knows exactly why.

Glossary

code
A set of laws.

collapse
To end suddenly.

embalm
To treat a body with chemicals so it won't decay.

eradicate
To fully get rid of something.

eruption
A sudden explosion, usually of a volcano.

functional
Something that works.

jackal
A type of wild dog.

marsh
An area of soft, low, wet ground usually covered with grasses.

mummify
To preserve a dead body.

ore
Metal mineral found in the ground.

phases
Stages the moon moves through (full, waning, waxing, and new).

platform
A flat surface.

route
A set way that many people travel.

stylized
Drawn or carved with simple details and not meant to look real or natural.

translate
To change from one language into another.

Read More

Felix, Rebecca. *Unearthing Early Human Remains.* Minneapolis, MN: ABDO Publishing, 2019.

Honovich, Nancy. *1,000 Facts about Ancient Egypt.* Washington, DC: National Geographic Kids, 2019.

Nardo, Don. *Ancient Mesopotamia.* Civilizations of the World. Lake Elmo, MN: Focus Readers, 2019.

Visit 12StoryLibrary.com

Scan the code or use your school's login at **12StoryLibrary.com** for recent updates about this topic and a full digital version of this book. Enjoy free access to:

- Digital ebook
- Breaking news updates
- Live content feeds
- Videos, interactive maps, and graphics
- Additional web resources

Note to educators: Visit 12StoryLibrary.com/register to sign up for free premium website access. Enjoy live content plus a full digital version of every 12-Story Library book you own for every student at your school.

Index

About the Author

Meg Marquardt started out as a scientist but likes writing about science even more. She enjoys researching physics, geology, and climate science. She lives in Madison, Wisconsin, with her two scientist cats, Lagrange and Doppler.

READ MORE FROM 12-STORY LIBRARY

Every 12-Story Library Book is available in many fomats. For more information, visit **12StoryLibrary.com**